MAKING YOUR OWN COMICS

STICK FIGURE CHARACTERS

All you need to tell a comic strip story are some basic stick people with blob-shaped bodies – just add a few details to turn them into characters.

Here are some examples of stick figure characters.

Elf

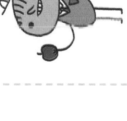

Surgeon

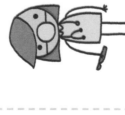

School student

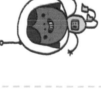

Astronaut

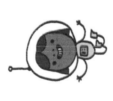

Superhero

Police officer

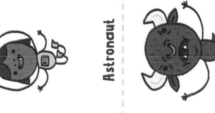

DJ

Minotaur

Here are some accessories you could use to create characters.

Add features, clothes and accessories to turn these stick figures into characters.

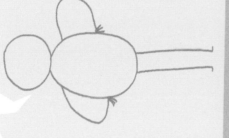

My secret identity is
_____

Job: _____
Loves: _____
Hates: _____

Hello, my name's
_____

Job: _____
Loves: _____
Hates: _____

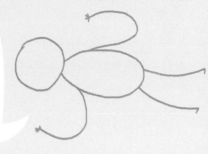

Some people call me
_____

Job: _____
Loves: _____
Hates: _____

I'm _____

Job: _____
Loves: _____
Hates: _____

DRAWING EXPRESSIONS

In comics, you can show a lot of different emotions using just a few simple lines.

Here are some different ways of drawing facial features.

Here are some simple expressions to copy.

Eyes

Noses

Mouths

Ears

Happy

Worried

Shocked

Sleepy

Humph!

Afraid

ARGH!

Delighted

Helpless laughter

heh he heh he heh...

Evil cackle

Hmmm?

Screaming

Sad

Puzzled

Crying

Nervous

Add details to the blank faces in the comic below, using the characters' expressions to tell the story.

How do you think the character feels about getting a present?

It's a snake! How do the two characters react?

Are they running away from the snake in fear? Or off for a fun jog with a new pet?

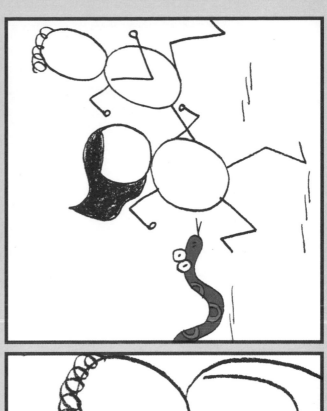

DRAWING BODIES

You can use simple shapes to create characters with very different body types.

Turn the rest of these shapes into characters of your own.

ACTION

Draw characters in action using some of these poses. You could put this page up somewhere so you can copy the poses for your other comics.

Use motion lines like this to show movement.

Walking

Skipping

Waterskiing

Jumping

Hanging on

Celebrating

Running

Crawling

Swimming

Dancing

Pointing

Falling

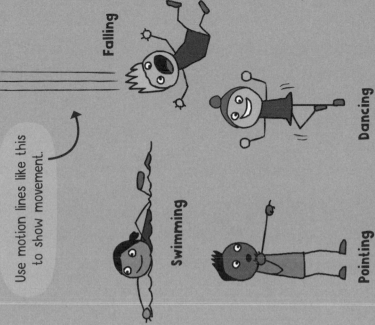

Draw a simple comic strip of some stick figures having a race. Who wins?

Draw the winner celebrating on this side of the finish line.

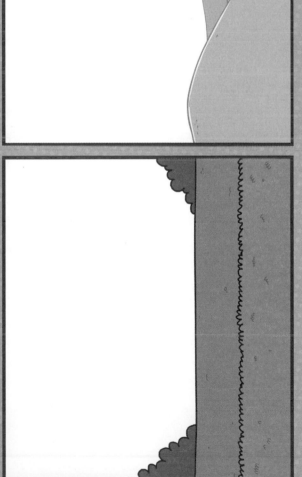

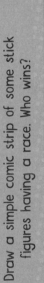

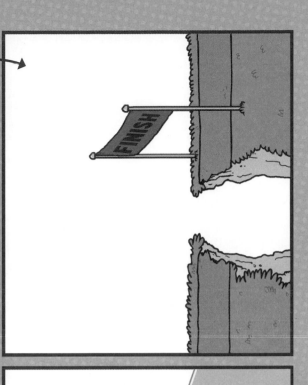

A SENSE OF PLACE

Here are some simple ways to show where your comic is set. Use some of these ideas to add backgrounds to the comic strip at the bottom of the page.

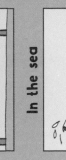
In bed

Desert at night

Going up stairs

In the sea

On a boat

A volcano!

In a car

Inside a house

Underwater

A scene in space

Tropical sunset

By a brick wall

In a forest

Street scene

In the mountains

Add three different backgrounds to these panels to show this stick person going from one place to another.

dum di dum

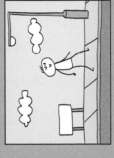
Well, I've never been HERE before!

Home sweet home!

You could pin this sheet up somewhere to give you background ideas when you're drawing other comics.

SPEECH AND SFX

To show speech and noises in comics, you need speech bubbles and sound effects, or SFX for short.

PAf FLAP TINKLE ROAR! PSSSST!

TICK TICK TICK **BEEP** WHIRRR PARP

SCRIBBLE TAP TAP TAP **KABOOOOOOM!**

WAAAAAAAAH! WHACK SCREEEECH! **SMASH**

Sound effects don't always have to be real words...

When it comes to speech bubbles, write the words, then draw the bubble around them.

Otherwise you might not have enough room.

Here are a few different types of speech bubbles you could use.

Voice coming through a phone, radio or loudspeaker.

Whispering

SHOUTING!

Thought bubble

Write SFX directly in the panel – no bubble needed.

VROOOOM!

Add speech bubbles and sound effects to this comic strip.

ACTION SEQUENCES

In comics, you can convey a sense of movement by spreading an action, such as walking across a room, over a few panels.

Superhero leaping

Cat jumping

Person swimming

Caterpillar crawling

Person running

With a repetitive action, you can return to the same pose again to complete it.

Draw a character carrying out a single action across these three panels to create your own action sequence.

CREATING A SHORT COMIC

To make a short comic with three panels, think of the panels as the beginning, middle and end of your story.

Pick a character and problem from the lists below and draw a comic strip in the blank panels.

Characters

★ Clumsy viking
★ Angry butterfly
★ Dog who's afraid of mice
★ Bossy monkey
★ Pirate who loves dancing

Eeek a mouse!

Problems

★ Monster attack
★ Spilling a hot drink
★ Arriving late for school
★ A huge tree falls over
★ Making an embarrassing mistake

Ways to vary how you show your characters in different panels

Coming in from the side. RAWWWR! 	Distance view Nooo! Get away!
Close up	Silhouette view Woo hoo!
From behind Oops!	Showing just one body part. I'm trapped!

Introduce your character here and draw a background.

Introduce a problem to make your character's life more complicated.

Solve the problem – or have your character fail, for an unhappy ending.

A SIX PANEL STORY

You can create a longer comic strip using a simple formula: in the first panel, draw something bad happening. Next, add something good that solves the problem, and so on...

Here are some good and bad things you could draw in the panels.

You're late!

Time machine

New shoes

CHEW

I'll save you!

Deep dark hole

HEEEEELP!

Something bad happens here.

Something makes the bad thing better.

A good thing

Another bad thing

One last, really bad bad thing

End your story on a good thing.

THE JOURNEY

Create a comic strip about a character going on a journey. Think about what might happen as your character travels through different places.

To show a character is asleep, fill a speech bubble with ZZZZZZZZZs.

Draw your character at the start of the journey. Write the destination on the signpost.

How does your character travel? What does the landscape look like?

Night falls. Draw your character taking shelter somewhere.

Hours later...

Your character meets a talking bear in a forest. What do they say to each other?

Something goes wrong before the end of the journey. How does your character react?

Does your character end up in the right place?

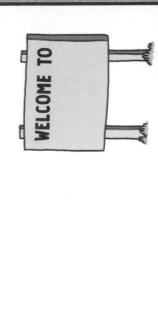

WELCOME TO

DETECTIVE COMIC

Create a comic strip about a detective solving a crime. There are some suggestions for what you could put in the panels along the way.

For a detective story you'll need

A detective
★ A police detective
★ A private investigator
★ A dog working with the Bone City Police

Suspects
These are the people the detective thinks might be guilty of the crime.

Clues
★ An object left behind by the criminal
★ Fingerprints or footprints
★ Strands of hair

A solution
You should work this out before you start drawing your comic.

Start by drawing the detective at the scene of the crime. Where is it? What's the crime?

Who does the detective think did it? Draw the number one suspect.

PRIME SUSPECT:

The detective finds a clue here...

Oh no, something goes wrong!

There's a chase! The criminal is running away!

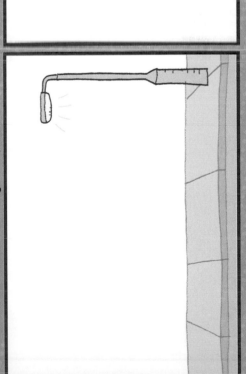

At last! The detective catches the criminal.

RULER FOR A DAY

Imagine being king or queen for the day. What orders would you give? What would you eat? What official duties would you perform?

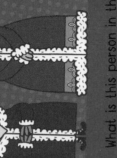

Some very royal drawing ideas

What do you eat for the royal breakfast?

9:30am

Your breakfast is served!

You're going to make a royal announcement. What will you say?

It's time to meet your public. Draw yourself waving from this balcony.

If you could ban one thing completely, what would it be?

Later...

What is this person in the crowd saying to you?

How would you end the day? With a palace ball? A secret meeting?

JOKE COMICS

Not all comics have to be funny, but an easy way to make a funny comic is to draw a strip based on a joke. The part that makes you laugh at the end of a joke is called the punchline. In a funny comic, put your punchline in the final panel.

Did you hear the one about the girl who put on a clean pair of socks every day?

By Friday she couldn't get her shoes on.

You could include silent panels, with actions but no words.

Draw your comic in these panels. Think about how to spread out the joke so you don't reach the punchline too soon.

Some other ideas to make your comic strips funny:

Adults behaving like babies.

Animals in clothes

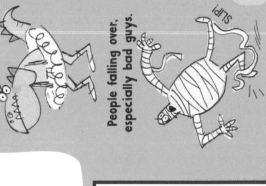

Characters making silly mistakes.

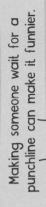

Oops, wrong bottle!

SOAP   DYE

People falling over, especially bad guys.

SLIP!

Making someone wait for a punchline can make it funnier.

...but YOU can milk it.

I don't know...

What do you call a cross between a shark and a cow?

SAVE THE PLANET

Planet Earth is in danger, but who can save it? This must be a job for... a superhero of your choice. Design your own superhero below to star in the comic on the right.

Name: _____

Powers: _____

Add a logo on your hero's chest.

What's threatening Planet Earth? Aliens? Meteors? A nuclear bomb?

BREAKING NEWS!

And now, news of Earth's almost certain doom...

Draw your superhero springing into action. What superpower is he or she using?

How does your superhero fight back against the villain?

Draw your superhero's arch-enemy trying to stop them from saving the world.

What does your superhero say to the grateful people of Earth?

Victory! Your superhero saves the world! How?

JUNGLE ANIMALS

Life in the jungle can be tough. Create a comic strip about the adventures of a small animal trying to find food without becoming food for someone else.

Some animals that could be your main character

Macaque

Tapir

I smell danger!

Lemur

Tree frog

Some predators (big scary flesh-eating animals) to run away from

Eagle

Jaguar

Python

Lemursssss? Deliciousssss!

Draw your animal character on the hunt for food.

The predator pounces!

Food found! But a predator is watching from between the leaves...

Does your animal run or fight?

What happens next?

Does your comic end happily for your animal?

A TRIP THROUGH TIME

To create a time travel adventure, pick a time period. Then, think about the mayhem people from the present could cause in that time, from bringing an object from the future with them, to preventing their own great-grandparents from meeting.

You could start your story with a time machine in the present.

Now draw the time and place the time machine travels to.

Times and places you could visit

Ancient Egypt

Pharaoh

16th-century Japan

Samurai

18th-century France

Aristocrat

Revolutionary

The Future

Spacesuits and clean energy jetpacks? Or a polluted nightmare?

MER-COMIC

What would it be like to live under the sea? Create a story about a mermaid or another undersea creature. What are the challenges of living underwater? What other sea creatures appear in your comic? Are they friendly? Helpful? Annoying?

Some characters you could use

Highly intelligent sea monster

Where am I?

Lost baby shark

When a character is breathing underwater, draw bubbles like this.

Lonely deep-sea fish

Everyone thinks I'm weird.

Enthusiastic teenage mermaid

Hair floats underwater

OMG! I just saw the BEST FISH EVER!

GRRR! ARRRGH!

Design a monster and draw a comic about its adventures. Does it live in a world of other monsters? Or does it live in our world?

Some monster ideas

Design your monster here:

PIRATE ADVENTURE

Set sail on a swashbuckling adventure! To create your own pirate comic, you could use some of the ideas on the right.

X marks the spot!

Telescope

Treasure map

Ship's wheel

Pirate ship

Ideas

★ Mutiny (rebelling against the captain)
★ Boarding a merchant ship with an unusual cargo
★ Finding treasure

★ Parrot insults the captain
★ Seasick cabin boy
★ Someone falls overboard
★ Shipwreck!

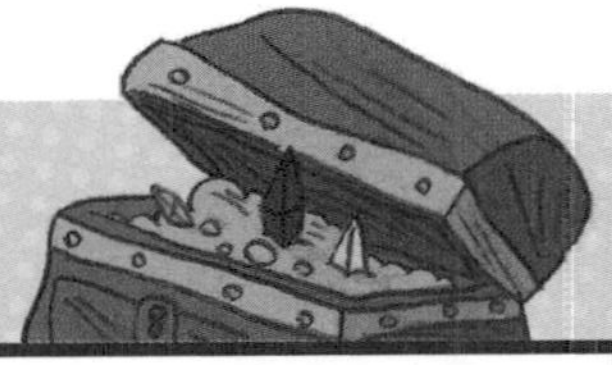

Rude parrot

The captain smells like weevils.

Captain

UNDERGROUND

You find a tunnel leading down beneath the street. Create a comic about where it might lead and what happens down there.

Who lives beneath the city? Intelligent moles? Goblins? Dinosaurs who've evolved into something else?

How do they react to you coming into their underground kingdom?

What do the people (or creatures) who live down there eat? What do they do all day? Who's in charge?

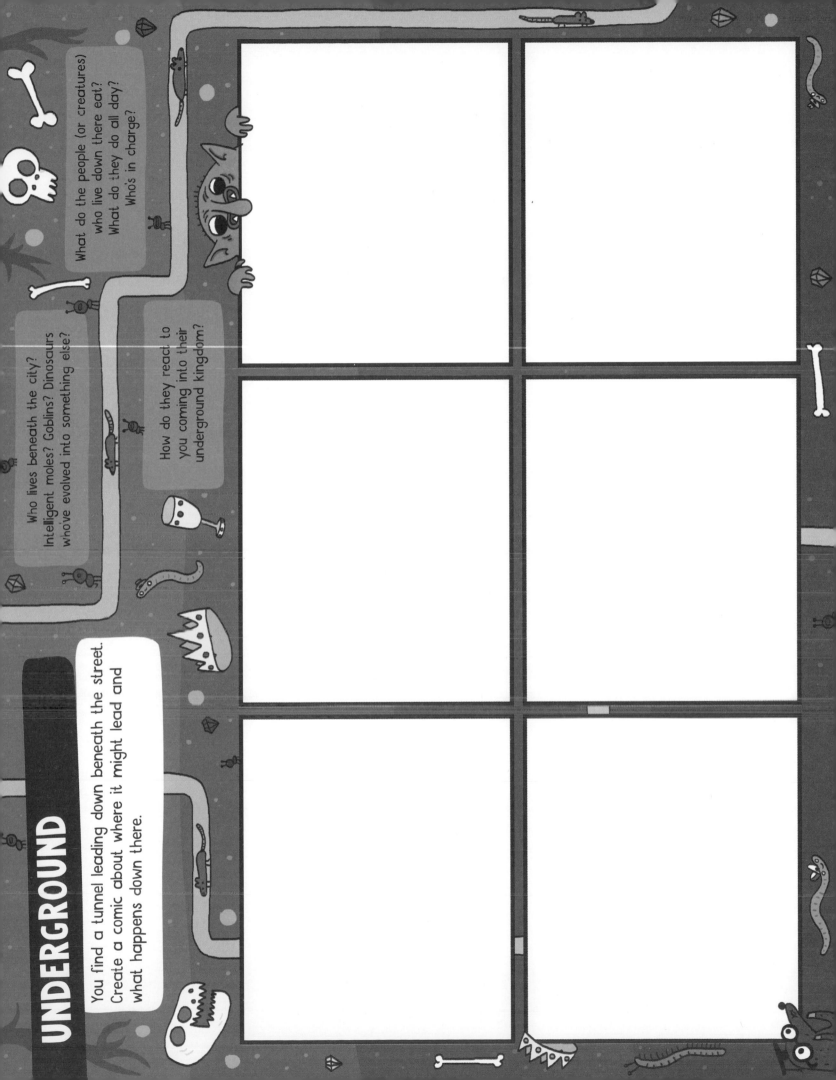

ON THE RUN

Create a comic strip about a character who's running away from someone or something. You could dress your character in various disguises.

Why is your character on the run? Maybe she or he...

★ is wanted by the police.

★ owns a magical object that supernatural villains want.

★ is a spy and enemy agents are in pursuit.

Ideas for disguises

Some places where your character could hide or try to blend in...

a cave in the wilderness

a circus

a parade

a film set

A NEW WORLD

A spacecraft full of brave explorers is heading from Earth to set up a colony on a new planet, many millions of light years away. What will the crew of explorers find when they arrive at their new home?

You could draw the explorers' spacecraft landing here.

You could note down some ideas about your characters and their new home here before you start your comic.

Spacecraft name: _____

Crew names: _____

Captain's name: _____

Alien life detected on planet? Yes ☐ No ☐

Atmosphere: Poisonous? ☐ **Breathable?** ☐

ROGUE ROBOT RAMPAGE

Create a comic about an inventor who builds a robot. What happens when the robot does NOT do what it's meant to do?

You could start your comic before the robot goes wrong...

...then introduce the malfunction here.

The robot is supposed to...

But actually it...

Does the inventor stop the robot? How?

IN DREAMS

Anything can happen in a dream. Draw a comic set in a dream, or based on a dream you've had.

Some ideas for strange things that could happen

A celebrity starts teaching at your school. What does she teach?

You can fly.

You've got to fight for your right to party.

Everything is made of cheese.

You meet an armadillo who tells you the meaning of life.

A CREEPY COMIC

Create a comic about your greatest fears. Insects? The dark? Ghosts? Monsters? A plague of locusts flying into your bedroom and swarming all over your face?

Try a black panel to show that someone's turned out the lights.

> Where's the light switch? Ah... there... but what's that slimy sound?

You could draw a scary character in shadow at first...

> *CLICK*
> W..what is it?

...revealing its true horror in the next panel.

RRRRRRRRR!

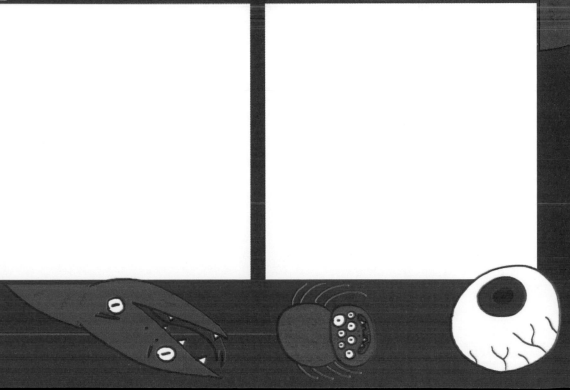

A QUEST COMIC

Create your own fantasy comic by picking a hero, a quest and some obstacles that get in the hero's way.

Quest ideas

★ Search for a magic cup
★ Defeat a dragon
★ Find the fountain of everlasting life
★ Rescue an elf prince

Obstacles

★ Evil dark lord
★ Trolls guarding a bridge
★ Poisonous berries
★ Really itchy shirt
★ Rival hero who is on the same quest as you

Is there a reward for completing the quest?

You could give your hero one final, huge obstacle here.

Pick a hero:

Crafty wizard

Anxious warrior

Arrogant elf

Plucky goblin orphan

CREATING A COVER

If you want to make one of your comics into a book, you could use this page to design the front cover.

Choose a short, snappy title.

Add your title in big letters. It could go at the top or the bottom.

Draw your main character doing something exciting, or in a dramatic pose.

HUNTED

Your name

Add your name in slightly smaller letters than the title.

Draw a background, or just give a hint of the setting for your comic.

Title: _____

Page number: _____

You could use this sheet to create a new comic, or finish one of the comics from earlier in the pad.

Title: ----------

Page number: ----------

You could use this sheet to create a new comic, or finish one of the comics from earlier in the pad.

HOW DO I DRAW...?

Here are some simple everyday things to draw in your comics — and some less everyday things too.

Animals

 goldfish

 dog

 sheep

bird

 penguin

crocodile

lion

cat

horse

Accessories and tools

tools

computers, phones and tablets

hats

bags and suitcases

Backgrounds and buildings

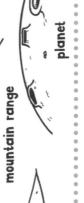 planet

mountain range

desert

trees

city

rolling hillsides

castle

Monsters and creatures

 goblin

vampire

werewolf

cyclops

winged horse

dragon

Inside a house

 bookshelves

table and chairs

toilet

bed

lamp

couch

Vehicles

 ferry

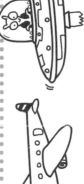 UFO

plane

rocket

car

helicopter

LOTS MORE COMICS TIPS

So, what next? Here are some tips to hep you keep on making amazing comics.

Try to vary the sizes of your panels and the way you lay out the page. Here are a few layouts to try.

The fewer panels on a page, the quicker the action will seem, because it takes less time to read.

Experiment with "silent" comics, with no speech bubbles or sound effects.

A huge panel, taking up a whole page, can be good for dramatic scenes with lots of characters.

Vary how you use text – for example, add words to posters in the background, or text messages on a character's phone.

To keep your lettering straight, you could rule lines in pencil, then write the words in pen, and erase the lines at the end.

Keep a sketchbook. It will help you improve your drawing, and you can dip back into it for ideas.

Sketch out a quick rough version of your comics, to make sure you like the way it's laid out, and that the story works.

Try creating a comic with a friend, with one person drawing the pictures, the other writing the words. (That's how many professional comics creators work.)

Don't pack too many words into your comic. Let the words – and the pictures – breathe a little.

Draw in pencil first, then go over the lines in black pen.

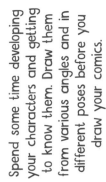

Spend some time developing your characters and getting to know them. Draw them from various angles and in different poses before you draw your comics.

Read comics to help you to understand how they work.

PLANETFALL

HAVE YOU SEEN THIS SUPERVILLAIN?